THE ZERO WASTE HOME

101 Ways To Reduce Waste & Save Money In Your Home

KATE ANDERSON

© 2015

Table Of Contents

Introduction: The Zero Waste Home

During our short time on Earth, human beings have made more of an impact than any other species and our footprint continues to grow. We inhabit 80% of the land on our planet and we have altered the vast majority of it. Our fellow animal species are suffering. Our air and water are forever changed. But it's not just the world around feeling the impact. We humans also suffer.

As time goes on, it's hard to ignore the fact that humans are creating more and more waste. These days landfills are overpacked with plastics, food waste, electronic devices, and even recyclable materials. Our waste disposal practices are causing contamination in our land, water systems, and the air we breathe. We have caused fundamental changes to the world around us not only affecting plants and animas, but also posing a serious threat to our own health.

We live in a world of take-away food, coffee-to-go, and a plethora of household disposables. Our convenience foods are over-packaged. Our plastic bags aren't just floating romantically in the breeze; they're releasing toxins into our land and water, harming thousands of animal species, and leaving our future generations starved of finite resources like petroleum and natural gas.

The fact is, we are still paying the price for the poor waste disposal practices of our ancestors, and f we're going to make a difference, we need to start making changes now. It's time to start taking care of our planet and teaching our children to do the same. If each of us make even a handful of changes to our every day lives, we can dramatically decrease the damage being caused to the environment.

Living in a No-Waste Home is far easier than most people think and it doesn't just help the planet, it can also save you heaps of money! This book is designed to show you and your family how to create less waste and save money. It is laid out in an easy-to-follow format so you can get the information you want quickly and get into action! I have laid out 101 simple tips and tricks that can make a big difference to the environment *and* your wallet!

This book covers how to reduce waste in every room in your home as well as when you and your family are out and about. I have included a special section on No-Waste Parenting and offered you some of my favorite craft projects to inspire you to turn your trash into treasure! But, before I move on to the good stuff, here's a few facts and figures about how human waste is affecting the world around us.

10 Facts About Waste
(More interesting than you might think, HONEST!)

1.) The average person generates around 1.5 tons of waste each year.

2.) Approximately 1/3 of food in the world goes to waste. American families lose around $600 per year from food waste alone.

3.) If worldwide food waste was reduced by just 15%, 25,000,000 people could be fed!

4.) Over 97% of food waste ends up in landfills where it breaks down and produces methane emissions which continue to be produced long after the landfill site is closed.

5.) Approximately two thirds of household waste is compostable. If this waste was simply composted rather than brought to landfills, it would form carbon dioxide rather than methane. This would cause considerably less harm to the environment.

6.) $1 out of every $10 spent on food is dedicated to packaging alone. These packages can take anywhere from 100 to 1,000,000 years to break down in landfills.

7.) It is estimated that less than 1% of plastic bags are recycled.

8.) Less than half of America's recyclable waste actually gets recycled.

9.) Various serious and chronic illnesses are caused by the pollutants created from improper waste disposal. Children are the most vulnerable group to be affected by these conditions.

10.) Every day items such as household cleaners and plastic packaging contain toxic chemicals that are causing detrimental effects in ecosystems around the globe. Switching to naturally produced or homemade cleaners would make a significant difference to the planet and could preserve the life of the plants and animals we share it with.

As a society, we have grown far too used to disposable items. We throw away packaging of all kinds and in great abundance. We clean with disposable wipes and single use paper products. We throw away clothes, toys, and books when we're done with them. We replace far more things than we reuse. The more "convenient" the world around us becomes, the more susceptible we are to take short cuts that will inevitably have a detrimental effect on our planet. And what's worse is that we're spending a fortune on things that end up in the trash often just minutes after purchasing them! It's time to make a change.

Most of us have heard of the 'The Tree R's': **reduce, reuse,** and **recycle** but very few of us are actually putting these ideals into practice. Although recycling is better than doing nothing, it's not enough to just recycle what we can. The real change comes from reducing and reusing. Here's why:

Reduce - Reducing how much you consume is the most effective of 'The Three R's'. Production of just about anything takes materials and energy; usually involving packaging and transport. By consuming more than you need - be it food, clothing, tools, toys, cleaning products, or virtually anything else - you could be causing unnecessary harm to the planet. Thus, whatever you buy too much of now, the next generation that will pay for. Making smart choices about how much your family consumes and reducing the amount of items you purchase means your household will produce less waste.

Reuse - Reusing items you're finished with rather than throwing them away is the second most effective 'R'. By giving your belongings a second (or third, or fourth...) life you won't contribute more waste to landfills and you could be simultaneously reducing the need for new products. Most of us reuse things without even noticing. For instance, if your child is too old for a toy, you might give it to a friend whose child will benefit from it. But reusing things shouldn't stop there. You can also reuse things by repurposing them. Getting into the habit of asking yourself "could I use this for something else?" before you throw something away is a habit that could greatly benefit both the planet and your wallet!

Recycle - Recycling is the least effective of 'The Three R's', although still an important one! Proper disposal of your recyclables is better than having them end up in landfills! However, recycling does use a considerable amount of energy and the process can produce pollutants. All in all, recycling is better than nothing but we can all do better than that.

Reducing Waste In The Kitchen

The kitchen is often thought of as the brain of the home. It's where we eat, socialize, and entertain. As such, it is our kitchens which produce the vast majority of household waste. Food waste in this day and age is at an all time high, causing irreparable damage to our planet, starving the population of food resources, and costing us each a small fortune in groceries and disposal costs. But it doesn't have to be this way! There are many things you can do to cut your kitchen waste down to almost nothing. The following list will show you a number of easy ways you can start making a difference.

22 Ways To Reduce Waste In The Kitchen Fast!

1.) Get A Few Meals Out Of One Ingredient

Most people's refrigerators are full of half-used and rotting fruits, vegetables, meats, cheeses, and other perishable items. A great number of this produce ends up being thrown away each week. Rather than letting all your fresh ingredients go bad, think ahead! When planning your meals for the week, don't choose 6 recipes that each require 20 different ingredients! Reduce waste and save money by planning two or more meals around each one ingredient. For instance, if you're buying a butternut squash to make a spicy curry, use half of it for your curry on Monday and turn the rest of it into a soup on Tuesday (*and* have the leftovers for lunch on Wednesday!). Or if you're planning on buying fresh mozzarella cheese for a Sunday lasagna and you expect to have some leftover, plan to make a pizza for a special Tuesday dinner or a salad caprice for Thursday lunch. What about that jar of pesto that's been sitting in the back of your fridge? It's probably ready to be thrown out now! But the next time you buy pesto, plan a few meals around it to make sure it doesn't end up in the trash!

2.) Use What You Have

We're all guilty of saying "there's nothing to eat!" from time to time. Sometimes we say it when we don't feel like cooking or we'd rather order in. Other times we say it when we genuinely can't figure out what to make because we're tired after a long day! The problem is, if you get used to ordering in and ignoring the ingredients in your cupboards, you're more likely to throw them away later in the week. Not to mention how much you'll spend on takeaway and how much packaging it comes in! So what's the answer when there's "nothing" to eat? Before you pick up the phone to call for pizza, take the No Shop Challenge! Challenge yourself to create a meal out of the ingredients you already have in the house and don't allow yourself to go to the shore for "top-up" items. Be creative! Ensure that there is always *something* to eat by keeping your cupboards stocked with dry goods and other long life items. This can be pasta, rice, beans, homemade pancake mix, whatever your family likes! You might have some leftover sauce or a few remaining veggies in the fridge that will bulk up your meal. You'll be surprised at how many meals you can come up with out of a few basic ingredients. So before you pick up the phone or head to the store, get creative in the kitchen and use what you've already got!

3.) Only Make As Much As You Need

This might sound obvious but if you regularly throw away leftovers, you're probably making too much food! If you're only cooking for one or two people, don't make enough for four! Cook only as much as you need. If you're following a recipe in a cookbook which serves 4 and there's only 2 of you, cut it in half. Similarly, don't fall into trends of cooking in bulk if you're unlikely to eat it! Making a large batch of soup and freezing it in single portions is a great idea, *if* you're actually going to eat it!

4.) Get The Most Out Of Your Bread

Depending on the size of your family and their appetite for bread, there are a number of ways to make sure you never throw stale bread in the trash again. If your loaf is likely to go bad before it gets eaten, put the amount you won't eat in the freezer. If you only use half a loaf of bread at a time, take out the amount you need when you first buy your loaf and freeze the rest. If you don't eat much bread at all, put the whole loaf in the freezer and just take a slice out when you need it and defrost it in your toaster or toaster oven. The same goes for pancakes, waffles, bagels, and any other bread product!

Top Tip: If you're freezing bagels, always cut them before you freeze them. That way you can put them straight in the toaster without having to wait for them to thaw.

Other things you can make with excess bread include homemade croutons, bread and butter pudding, French toast, or breadcrumbs for use in your favorite recipes! For extra flavor to your breadcrumbs by adding some fresh or dried herbs like oregano, basil, thyme, or sage. Throw some sea salt and black pepper in there too. And of course, if you won't use your breadcrumbs before they go bad, pop them in the freezer for another time!

5.) Get The Most Out Of Your Fruit

If you have a lot of fruit that needs used quickly, there are plenty of things you can do to make sure it doesn't go to waste. Most fruit can be frozen and used at a later date. To freeze berries or grapes, place them on a baking tray in the freezer (this keeps them from getting stuck together). Once they're frozen, put them into an air tight freezer bag. The same method can be used for apple slices. Use your frozen fruit for smoothies or to liven up your pancakes or homemade muffins!

If it's bananas you have too many of, make banana bread or add a mashed banana into some pancake mix to add a natural sweetness to your breakfast. Alternatively, freeze your bananas whole and simply squeeze them out of their skin to use for baking or smoothies at a later date!

Top Tip: Most berries and grapes are only in season during the summer months. Save money by stocking up at the end of the season while berries are still cheap and freeze them to use in autumn and winter.

6.) Get The Most Out Of Your Vegetables

There are quite a few things you can do to get the most out of your veggies. When preparing meals take all of the trimmings from your fresh veggies (carrot peels, celery hearts, mushrooms, onion offcuts, radishes, herb stems, etc.) and pop them in your freezer in a large clip top jar. Every time you cook, add your trimmings to that jar in the freezer. When your jar is full, make your own vegetable stock by putting the trimmings in the large pot, covering them with water, and adding a few spoonfuls of salt. Simmer for an hour, sieve, and cool. Then freeze your stock in ice cube trays to use in future cooking!

For other veggies that are close to expiration, make soup, stews, baby food, or a delicious healthy juice. Alternatively, if you know you won't get a chance to use them, throw those veggies in the jar with your trimmings to buff up your homemade stock!

7.) Get The Most Out Of Your Dairy Products

Quite a few dairy products can be frozen including milk and cheese! If you have a block of cheese you won't use before it expires, grate it and sprinkle with a spoonful of corn starch to keep it from clumping. Spread it out on a baking sheet and stick it in the freezer. When it's frozen, sweep the cheese into a freezer bag and use it for homemade pizza, lasagne, quesadillas, or a casserole. And what about all those recipes that call for 1/3 of a cup of buttermilk? Next time you buy a carton of buttermilk, instead of throwing it away after you use the 1/3 cup, freeze it for next time!

8.) Pack Your Lunches And Snacks

Packing your lunch really can save you a lot of waste and money! Get the most out of your dinners by packing your leftovers for tomorrow's lunch. Invest in some <u>good quality tupperware</u> which is perfect for storing food both in the home and on the go. Make sure your fresh fruits don't go to waste by washing them and packing them into lunchbox size portions when you first buy them. Do this at the start of your week so you don't put pressure on yourself during the morning household rush. Do the same with pretzels, cheese and crackers, berries, and other perishables. Remember to always use washable containers instead of disposable sandwich bags and food wraps.

9.) Get More Out Of Baking

There are a number of ways you can use your freezer to benefit you when it comes to baked goods. Muffins, cookies, sweet breads, and cupcakes can all be frozen after baking. This is good news for all that banana bread you make with your over-ripe bananas! Simply store your baked goods in an airtight container, label them with the date, and freeze until the next time you're expecting company or you need something fun for your lunch box. For cupcakes, freeze before icing them. Take them out of the freezer and let them thaw for a few hours or overnight. Put frosting on them in the morning.

When you're baking cookies, only bake the amount that you need. Take any leftover dough and press it into a sausage shape. Wrap the dough with plastic wrap and stick it in the freezer. The next time you want to make cookies, avoid the time, energy, and mess by simply cutting your frozen dough into 1/2 inch slices and bake as usual.

10.) Reduce Waste On Special Diets

In many households, there is someone who eats differently than the rest of the family. This may be because of an allergy or lifestyle choice or you may just have a picky eater on your hands. This is very common but not always easy to cater for. If you're making two meals every dinner time you're bound to feel under pressure, spend more time and money than you need to, *and* create more waste.

Try these 3 tips to save waste with special diets:

*Plan everyone's meals in advance. Plan meals for your special dieter around the produce you're already purchasing for the rest of the family.

*Plan meals that will suit everyone. For instance, if you have a vegetarian in your home, make a vegetarian meal the whole household will enjoy. If your special eater can't have gluten, use a gluten-free recipe for the whole family rather than wasting time and money making separate meals for everybody.

*Use your freezer wisely! Divide the leftovers from your special dieter's meal into individual portions and freeze them for a later date.

11.) Keep Perishables At The Front Of Your Cupboards

In order to get the most out of your fresh foods, always store them at the front of your refrigerator and cupboards so you remember to use them before they go out of date. Keep your dried and canned goods at the back. This is an easy way to make sure you get the most out of groceries you may have otherwise forgotten about.

12.) Keep It Airtight

Keep your food fresh by storing it correctly. Rather than allowing your food to sit in an open bag, store flour, sugar, dried fruit, nuts, cereals, and other dried goods in airtight containers or glass jars. This will keep them fresh and safe from unwanted house guests like bugs and mice.

13.) Think Twice Before You Throw It Out

There are a lot of things we regularly throw away that could be useful. You can reduce your waste and save money by reusing things you would normally throw out. Not only can you use jars and other lidded containers for food storage but almost any "trash" could be useful in the future. For instance, cereal boxes, tin foil, tissue paper, and paper towel rolls might be useful for arts and crafts projects like stenciling, modeling, or other school projects. Small plastic tubs from yogurts or pudding can be used as paint pots. Plastic containers from things like berries or mushrooms can be used to grow herbs in. Rubber bands and string might also come in handy later! Use your bread bags for sandwich or snack bags! Get into the habit of questioning anything you're about to throw away.

14.) Reuse Your Coffee Grounds

Used coffee grounds have a variety of household and kitchen functions. First of all, they are great for absorbing odors. Put a small dish of used coffee grounds in the back of your refrigerator instead of buying baking soda every time your fridge needs freshened up. Do the same in your bathroom. You can also use your coffee grounds on a sponge to remove grease from pots and pans, maple syrup spills from your kitchen counters, or dried-on cereal milk from your dining table. If you have a garden, a back yard, or an outdoor container garden, sprinkle your used coffee grounds in and around your plants to fertilize them and keep bugs away.

15.) Compost

Composting food and other garden waste is the best possible way to deal with it. Depending on where you live, your city council may provide you with a compost bin for your food and garden waste. If your council does not offer this service, consider composting your food at home. This may not be an option if you have no outdoor space but if you think composting might be an option for you, give it a try! If you do any gardening or know someone else who does, your compost will come in handy in the future.

16.) Use Reusable Storage Methods

Using a lot of plastic wrap, tin foil, or sandwich bags, and other disposable packaging creates quite a lot of waste; most of which is not biodegradable. Use reusable storage methods such as jars and other lidded containers wherever possible.

17.) Reuse Sandwich Bags

If you have to use <u>sandwich bags</u>, reuse them any time you can. For instance, if you stored something like pretzels or peanuts in a sandwich bag, you might use that bag again for screws, nails, or arts and crafts supplies. If your child's lunch box had a bag of grapes in it, simply refill it for tomorrow. Think outside the box! Before you throw something away, ask yourself if it can be used again or if it might serve a purpose later.

18.) Use Cloth Napkins

Say no to paper napkins! Purchase some cloth napkins for your every day family use and when you're entertaining guests. Not only will you save waste and money, but you'll also find that cloth napkins can absorb much more. That means mopping up spills will be much easier and more efficient.

19.) Re-Use Egg Cartons

Egg cartons can almost always be used again. Cardboard cartons can be used for planting seeds. They are degradable so when your seedling appears you can simply plant it - carton and all - into the next size plant pot. This will eliminate all waste! Plastic egg cartons can be used for kids' arts and crafts projects or paint pallets. If you live near someone with a hen farm, offer them your egg cartons to be reused.

20.) Say No To Processed Foods

There are a multitude of reasons you should avoid buying and eating pre-packaged processed foods. Firstly, they are bad for your health! Most "convenience" foods are packed with sugar, salt, fat, and other low quality ingredients. Furthermore, they use more packaging than any other food products. And lastly, they cost a fortune! The best way you can avoid these foods is by cooking at home using whole foods and storing leftovers in the freezer for when you don't have time to cook. If cooking isn't your forte, challenge yourself to learn a few simple recipes from a cookbook, the internet, or a friend! It's easier than you think!

21.) Make A Donation

If you have canned or dried goods that you won't use, donate them to a local charity, a school can drive, or a friend or relative that could use them! Do everything you can to make sure your food items do not end up in the trash.

22.) Recycle

If you cannot reuse or repurpose something make sure you recycle wherever possible. Recycling takes energy and materials but it is still much better than the production of new things made from raw materials.

In many homes, excess waste can be reduced dramatically by simply putting more thought into shopping. Waste from food and food packaging makes up the majority of household waste. You can reduce your family's wastage by following a few simple shopping rules.

12 Rules For Smart Shopping

1.) Plan Your Meals

One of the best things you can do to reduce waste and keep your grocery costs down is to plan ahead. Decide on 5 to 7 dinners you'll have time to cook throughout the week and put the ingredients on your shopping list. Be realistic about your cooking plans. If you know you'll have limited cooking time on certain days, don't expect to do a three hour long cooking session. Always keep ingredients for one or two easy meals in your kitchen incase of very busy days or unexpected changes to your schedule. Write down what you will need for lunches and snacks for your whole family for the week. Use the same lunch and snack ingredients for the whole family where possible to avoid spending extra money.

When you're shopping, stick to your list! I cannot stress this enough. Do not get distracted by sales or other things you don't need or didn't budget for, *especially* perishables. Try not to take every member of the family to the grocery store with you so you can make sure you only buy what's necessary.

Top Tip: If you know you're particularly susceptible to sale shopping or you can't manage to get to the store without bringing your kids along, buy your groceries online so you can be sure you'll stick to your list. Always opt out of shipping packaging where possible.

2.) Take Stock

Before you do your grocery shopping, take stock of what you already have in your kitchen. Check your perishables and your dried and canned goods. Check your cleaning supplies and toiletries. If you've taken stock at home, you'll your shopping list will reflect it. Now instead buying bananas or milk 'just in case' you'll know if you actually need them. This means you won't end up buying more than you need and throwing them away later in the week. For the same reason, try not to pop into the grocery store without a list. Often when we're in the store, our eyes begin to wander and we might buy 10 things instead of the 3 things we popped in for!

3.) Go Light On Perishables

Be careful when purchasing perishables such as dairy and fresh fruit. Only buy the things you've planned to buy and will definitely use. Choose loose produce so you can control the amount you're buying. Beware of sales like buy one, get one free, or 3 for 2 on perishables as you may end up with more waste in the end.

4.) Be Smart About Sales

Grocery stores make a large portion of their profits by putting things on special offer. And it's hard to say no to a good bargain! However, in-store offers might encourage you to spend money on products you don't need which may go out of date before you get a chance to use them. Whenever you see something that's "buy one get one free" or "3 for 2" don't lose your head! Only take advantage of sales when you were already going to buy the product or when you are sure it will not go to waste. For instance, take advantage of sales on dried or canned goods that you regularly use, or cash in on sales on family favorites such as peanut butter, cereals, or crackers, but avoid sales on dairy, fruit, and vegetables unless they were already on your list. If something on your list happens to be included in a "3 for 2" offer, make sure you actually need 3 before buying 3! If you only need one and you buy three, you're spending more money than necessary and you might end up throwing the extra 2 away!

5.) Always Use Reusable Bags

An outstanding amount of plastic bags are thrown away every year causing serious harm to the environment and thousands of animal species. Avoid adding more plastic bags to landfills and water sources by always using reusable bags. Use canvas bags or boxes for your groceries. If you don't have your bag with you, ask yourself if you really need one before taking one at the store. If you only have a few items and you're just walking around the corner or to the car, carry your things in your arms rather than taking plastic bags.

6.) Buy In Bulk

Buying your food in bulk doesn't just mean buying a large supply so you don't run out. It also means reducing unnecessary packaging. Nowadays there are plenty of stores and markets where you can purchase your dried goods like nuts, beans, grains, fruits and vegetables, dairy and meat products, and even cereals and sweets in the amount you want rather than buying a smaller pre-packaged amount. This will save you an unbelievable amount of packaging and a considerable amount of money! Don't forget to bring your own jars, containers, or cloth bags to store your bulk goods in!

7.) Shop At The Farmer's Market

Market shopping is a fantastic way to purchase food without unwanted plastic packaging. Like buying in bulk, you only buy the amount of you need rather than ending up with rotten fruit and veggies a few days later. Furthermore, most sellers at the market will be happy for the return of plastic bags, fruit cartons, honey and jam jars, and egg cartons so you can bring your packaging back and be sure that it will be used again. The best thing is, the farmer's market can make for a great day out for the family and a great way to teach your children about environmentally friendly shopping!

8.) Go For Paper Packaging

If you have to buy pre-packaged foods or cleaning products, choose those that are packaged with paper or cardboard rather than plastic. For instance, choose dishwashing tablets in a cardboard box or bar soap wrapped in paper rather than liquid detergents in plastic bottles.

9.) Avoid Individually Wrapped Food Products

There are hundreds of food products wrapped in individual size portions for lunch boxes and easy travelling. These products produce a lot of unnecessary waste and cost a small fortune! Say no to pre-portioned foods and simply portion them out at home. You'll reduce a lot waste and save money.

10.) Invest In A Reusable Water Bottle

If you regularly buy small bottles of water, it's time to get one you can reuse! Get a water bottle that you like and either fill it with tap water or purchase mineral water in bulk and fill your bottle from that. Do the same for your children. Instead of contributing the mass of juice boxes in landfills, let your child choose a reusable bottle they like and use it for their favorite drinks at school or when you're out for the day.

11.) Get A Reusable Coffee-To-Go Cup

There is a staggering amount of takeaway coffee cups being thrown away each day around the globe. Make a stand by purchasing a reusable to-go cup. Most coffee shops will be happy to use your cup rather than a paper cup. So whether you fill your cup at home or have your favorite barista fill it for you, you'll be making a difference! Encourage your friends to do the same!

12.) Be Prepared

Many times we don't plan on going shopping but we end up popping to the store for one or two things. It's these times you're likely to have forgotten to bring your reusable bags. Be prepared for spontaneous shopping and other spontaneous events by keeping a shopping bag, a coffee cup, a reusable water bottle, and a cloth napkin in your car or at the office. Always keep a small reusable shopping bag in your purse just in case.

As I mentioned before, reducing and reusing are the most effective of 'The Three R's'. So far you've learned a number of ways to put these important R's into action. Remember to think of everything you purchase as having a future purpose. There are a number of ways you can reuse and repurpose glass jars from jams and sauces, plastic containers from your local takeaway, and spray bottles from cleaning products. The next list shows you some great ideas of how to turn your trash into treasure.

12 Ways to Re-use Jars and Containers

1.) Food storage
Instead of using plastic wraps, aluminum foil, or sandwich bags,
store your cooked foods, dried goods, herbs and spices, snack mixes,
and granola in your repurposed glass jars. They're handy, they'll
keep your foods fresh for longer, and they look stunning in your
kitchen!

2.) Candle Holders
Glass jars make ideal candle holders. You can decorate them with
fabric or glass paint or just use them as they are. To remove wax
from jars when your candles are used up, simply pour boiling water
into the jar, let it sit overnight, and the wax will float to the top so
you can remove it in one easy swoop!

3.) Odor Absorber
Fill a jar half full with used coffee grounds or baking soda and cover
with a small piece of cloth. Place it in your refrigerator or bathroom
to neutralize bad odors. Replace the coffee grounds or baking soda
every 3-4 weeks.

4.) Cocktail Shakers And Glasses
Having a cocktail party at home? Why not repurpose your jars and
use them as cocktail shakers and quirky drinking glasses? You'll
have a great time and create the perfect platform to talk to your
guests about reducing waste!

5.) Gifts
There are a number of homemade gift projects that your glass jars
could come in handy for. Homemade candles, jams and preserves,
granola, candy, and cookies make lovely gifts. Package them in your
repurposed glass jars, top them with piece of fabric and string, and

always encourage your loved ones to reuse the jar when they're finished with it!

6.) Flower Vases And Plant Pots

Decorate your old glass jars with fabrics or paint and put some freshly cut flowers in them for a subtle center piece. Or use your jars, containers, and disposable packaging tubs as planters for your favorite house plants and other gardening needs. Put a few stones at the bottom of your plant jars to ensure drainage for your plant.

7.) Homemade Party Favors

Have a wedding or birthday party coming up? Why not get crafty and personalize your glass jars for your guests? Whether all your jars are uniform or each is slightly different, party favours can brighten up any get together! If you don't have a special event coming up but you know someone who does, offer your jars to them!

8.) Reuse Takeaway Containers

If your takeaway food comes in reusable plastic containers, keep them and use them for leftovers or repurpose them as drawer organizers. If you frequently buy takeaway food, consider bringing your plastic container back to your favorite establishment and ask them to package your meal in it again. Doing this might just inspire other diners to do them same!

9.) Travelling Food

Next time you're going to a friend's house for lunch or packing a family picnic, use glass jars instead of plastic wraps, sandwich bags, or tinfoil. If you're giving food to a friend, encourage them to continue reusing the jar once they're finished with it.

10.) Repurpose Your Wine Bottles

You can use your empty wine bottles for a bunch of creative projects around the house. Make your own infused dipping oils and store them in a clean bottle. Decorate your bottle and use it as a vase for long stem roses, eucalyptus, or pussy willow. Or use your wine bottle in place of a rolling pin! If you have no purpose for your bottles, donate them to a local wine maker. They'll accept your donation gratefully!

11.) Reuse Your Spray Bottles
Keep your empty spray bottles from store bought cleaning supplies and use them for new homemade cleaners! Alternatively, ensure the bottles are thoroughly clean, and use them to spray your houseplants with fresh water.

12.) Make A Donation
If you have no use for your glass jars, donate them to someone who can use them such as a crafty friend or a local honey farmer.

Top Tip: To remove stubborn labels from glass jars, combine 1 part coconut oil and 1 part baking soda. Saturate the label with the mixture, leave to rest for an hour, then peel off. Scrub excess glue off with a scouring sponge.

Some of the most environmentally threatening household waste comes from cleaning products. Many chemical based cleaners are toxic to animals, water sources, and even humans. Reduce your household cleaning waste with the following ideas.

6 Simple Ways To Reduce Cleaning Waste & Save Money

1.) Say No To Disposable Wipes And Paper Towels
The majority of household cleaning chores can be done without the use of paper towels and disposable wipes. Replace your wipes with reusable metal scourers, brushes, and sponges. Instead of getting rid of your old towels and t-shirts, cut them into rags and use them in place of paper towels. You'll save a fortune on disposable items and you'll reduce your household waste considerably.

2.) Make Your Own
The best way to save money on cleaning products and reduce waste is to make your own cleaning products at home. Keep your spray bottles from other cleaners and mix up your own natural cleaners. You can make simple all-purpose cleaning sprays with lemon juice, vinegar, water, baking soda, and essential oils. Laundry detergent can also be easily made at home using natural products in place of chemicals. Doing this will reduce waste, save money, and prevent toxic household cleaners from coming into contact with your family or harming the planet.

3.) Buy In Bulk
If you're not keen on making your own detergents, buy your favorite dishwasher or laundry cleaners in bulk to save packaging. To avoid spending more money than necessary, look out for your favorite bulk items on sale and cash in while you can! When you're finished, refill or recycle the packaging. Remember: only buy things in bulk if you will definitely use them and choose cardboard packaging over plastic whenever possible.

4.) Say Goodbye To Air Fresheners
Most air fresheners are full of toxins and unwanted packaging. Replace aerosol cans and other sprays with homemade odor absorbers made from used coffee grounds (see above) and burn

essential oils to keep the air in your home smelling fresh. There are a number house plants which help purify air as well such as ferns, palms, spider plants, and peace lilies so keep a few of these in your home to ensure clean air for you and your family.

5.) Modify Your Laundry Habits
Washing machines use a lot of energy which can mean higher electricity bills and more strain on the environment. You can make your laundry habits more efficient in a number of ways. Start by only using your washing machine when you have a full load rather than doing a few small loads each week. Use the cold setting on any items that don't need to be sterilized (cold water is better for stains anyway!). Use shorter cycles for items that aren't badly soiled and avoid the use of a dryer wherever possible.

6.) Just Use *Less*
The quickest and easiest way you can reduce waste and save money on cleaning products is to simply use less of them. When cleaning, use only as much as you *need* to clean something. You might be using twice as much toilet cleaner or dish soap than necessary. Or you might be using far more detergent than your laundry actually requires! The next time you're cleaning try using a little bit less of your cleaning products and see how the results are. If you're satisfied with the results, try reducing the amount even further next time.

Reducing Waste In The Rest Of Your Home

Now that your kitchen is a fully functioning No-Waste room, it's time to focus on the rest of your home and start tightening up the screws! You should now have a good eye for reducing, reusing, repurposing, and recycling and you've probably come up with a few of your own waste reducing tricks by now. In this section and the sections that follow, I'm going to give you some of my favorite ways to reduce waste around the home including what to do with old towels, clothing, and paper products, how to deal with general waste, and how to be a No-Waste Parent. Then it's on to some fun ideas for craft projects made entirely of repurposed materials.

10 Ways To Get More Out Of Clothing, Towels, And Bedding

1.) Sell Up
If your clothes still have a lot of life left in them, list them for sale online or bring them to a consignment shop. This way you'll make some money toward new clothes and your clothing will be passed on to someone else in need. Remember to do the same with your baby and children's clothes!

2.) Make A Donation
The best thing you can do with clothes and towels that are in good condition is donate them to charity or pass them on to someone you know who can use them. This means they won't end up in landfills and someone else will benefit from them. Towels and bedding that are old or stained can be donated to animal shelters and other animal rescue institutions.

3.) Mend What You Can
If you have some articles of clothing that could do with some sprucing up, try mending them before getting rid of them. Small rips

and tears, missing buttons, and other alterations could extend the life of your clothing ensuring less waste and money saved.

4.) Make Some Cleaning Rags
Towels and clothing that have reached the end of their lifespan due to age, rips and tears, or stains make the perfect material for cleaning rags. Cut up towels are great for heavy cleaning jobs in the bathroom and mopping up spills on your floor. Tee shirts and other soft, light fabrics make fantastic dusters for your furniture and other surfaces.

5.) Use Hand-Me-Downs
If you have more than one child or you know someone with a child that's younger than yours, pass your kids' clothes down the line. Children grow very fast and they often grow out of their clothes and shoes long before they show signs of wear. Remember that children don't have to look fashionable at all times. It's good to have some clothes they can be comfortable and get dirty in. And don't forget, adults can benefit from hand-me-downs too!

6.) Cut Out Compulsive Buying
Many of us own far more clothing than we need, or in fact, that we actually wear. Compulsive clothes shopping costs money and ultimately, when your clothing goes out of style, it turns to waste. Cut out your compulsive buying by only buying clothes when necessary. Plan your shopping outings so as not to get sucked in by sales or impulse buying. Lastly, only buy clothes you know you will definitely wear.

7.) Be A Conscientious Shopper
When purchasing clothing, towels, or bedding, always bring your own bags and opt out of tissue paper and other unnecessary packaging.

8.) Reuse Your Odd Socks

Most households have a mound of odd socks lying around which never find their match and eventually get thrown away. Get creative with your odd socks by tying them together and making a rope toy for your dog. Or make sock puppets with the kids. Play a game of indoor "ice hockey" with the kids by putting on lots of socks and sliding around the living room. Make a glove style duster for polishing your furniture. Think outside the box!

9.) Reuse Old Stockings

Tights and pantyhose make great drawer fresheners, spice bags, and bird feeders so when your stockings are no longer wearable, get crafty!

10.) Reuse Your Bedding

Sheets and duvet covers can be used in many ways. If they're getting old you can use them as a picnic blanket. Or, if they're in good condition but don't suit your bedroom, think about making a table cloth or some cloth napkins with them. Use your baby's bedding to make a keepsake pillow for them. Challenge yourself to repurpose things wherever possible.

Now it's time to start thinking about your paper wastage. Remember that reducing and reusing are more effective than recycling. Are you getting the most out of your paper products? Have a look at the following tips about reducing paper waste in your home.

5 Ways To Tackle Paper Products

1.) Reuse It!
Single-sided paper can always be used again. You can use it for
scrap paper for children to draw on, homework study sheets, or
brainstorming ideas. Or cut the paper into strips and staple them
together to use for shopping or to-do lists. You can even attach a
magnet to the back and keep it on your refrigerator.

2.) Say Goodbye To Paper Bills
Paper bills are very wasteful as they take materials and energy to
produce *and* transport. Most utility and other bills are not necessary
to have in paper form. Most companies have an option to sign up for
e-bills. Doing so can reduce your paper waste dramatically. And if
you happen to need a bill in print, you can print it out at home or in
the library and at least eliminate the envelope and other materials.

3.) Say No To Junk Mail
If your mailbox is over flowing with catalogues, marketing flyers,
and takeaway restaurant menus, put a stop to it by putting a sign on
your door or mailbox that says "NO JUNK MAIL". You don't have
to put up with wasteful advertising.

4.) Rethink Magazine And Newspaper Subscriptions
Magazines and Newspapers use a lot of paper which usually ends up
being thrown away or recycled. Furthermore, they take energy to
transport them to your door. Consider changing your paper
subscriptions to electronic subscriptions and read your favorite
publications online. Alternatively, consider reading your favorite
magazines and newspapers at a local library. If you want to keep
your paper subscriptions, think about donating them when you're
finished with them or let your kids use them for school projects. You
an also use your newspapers when packaging goods for the post or to
clean your windows with some white vinegar. Or pass them on to a

friend with a puppy in training. If you know someone who is moving, offer them your newspaper to pack their glassware with!

5.) Buy Recycled Goods
Choose brands of toilet paper, tissues, and other paper products that are made using recycled materials. The energy it takes to make these items is less harmful to the environment than those made from raw materials.

Now that your No-Waste Home is really taking shape, it's time to take a look at the less obvious waste in your home including bulky and expensive items like furniture, electronics, and other elusive waste makers.

7 Ways To Reduce General Household Waste

1.) Upcycle - Before you send your old furniture to the dump, think about "upcycling" it. Many times all a piece of furniture needs is a new coat of paint or some reupholstering to make it like new again. If you have no use for your furniture, donate it to someone who can refurbish it to give it a new life rather than letting it pile up in the dump.

2.) Treat Your Belongings Nicely - By maintaining things like your car and other appliances you can ensure they will have a longer life. Taking care of your furniture and other items like bicycles, office equipment, and electronics is a great way of reducing waste and saving money.

3.) Use Rechargeable Batteries - Replace disposable alkaline batteries with rechargeable ones for your remote controls and kid's toys. Why use disposables when you don't have to?

4.) Be A Borrower - Before buying something new, ask yourself if you could rent or borrow it from a friend or library instead. The production of new things takes up materials, energy, and money. Why buy something new if you can simply borrow it and pass it on to someone else instead?

5.) Reuse Postal Packaging - Keep the packaging from any parcels you get in the mail and reuse it the next time you're sending in the mail! Most packaging is made from plastic and it can almost always be reused. Keeping things like newspaper and bubble wrap will also come in handy if you're moving or storing breakables.

6.) Use Natural Heating And Cooling Methods - Keep your home at a comfortable temperature without the use of air conditioning and heating systems whenever possible. Invest in draft excluders and heavy curtains in the winter. Keep interior doors closed to reduce drafts and when you're done cooking leave your hot oven open to help heat your home. In the summer use drapes and blinds to stay cool and keep windows and doors open for a natural breeze rather than turning on the air conditioner. If you'll be out for the day or you're planning a vacation away, turn your heating and cooling systems off until you return.

7.) Donate Electronics - Donate electronic items such as computers, printers, game consoles, and telephones to charities, schools, or libraries. Alternatively pass them on to a friend or relative. If your electronics are broken, give them to someone who can repair or refurbish them rather than throwing them away.

Reducing Waste With Babies And Children

If you have a baby or older children in your home, you have probably noticed an increase to your household waste. Children have special needs. Diapering and baby food makes up a large percentage of their contribution to waste, and as they continue to grow, and their capacity for making messes increases, children may create more waste than adults! School work, dirty clothing, and hobbies can make for an immense amount of household waste. In this next list, I'm going to show you some easy ways to be a No-Waste Parent.

12 Tips For No-Waste Parenting

1.) Breastfeed
Breastmilk isn't just convenient and healthy for you and your baby; it also reduces the need for cleaning and sterilizing bottles, heating formula, and disposing of packaging and chemical cleaners. Breastfeeding is free and eliminates the financial and environmental costs of energy and materials.

2.) Use Cloth Diapers
It's no secret that disposable diapers cost a shocking amount of money and wastage. But many people don't know that using cloth diapers is easier than it was a few decades ago! Washable diapers these days are well fitted, easy to clean, and just as easy as disposables when you're on the go. Furthermore, if you have more than one child, your cloth diapers can be passed down to the next baby!

3.) Say No To Baby Wipes
Baby wipes are very convenient but create an abundance of waste! Reduce the amount of baby wipes you're using by using reusable wipes with a bit of water on them. For messy hands and faces, use a washcloth or small towel which can be washed and used again. Remember to pack washcloths and towels in your changing bag!

4.) Make Your Own Baby Food

Pre-packaged baby food may be convenient but it comes with a ton of packaging. This means your baby food could nearly double your household food waste! What's more is that even organic store bought baby food is packed with preservatives and other additives like sugar and salt. Making your own baby food at home is simple and can cut wastage down to nil. It's easy to travel with *and* good for baby!

5.) Be Smart About Lunch

If you have a school aged child and who takes a packed lunch to school, always use a reusable lunch box rather than disposable paper or plastic bags. Steer clear of individually wrapped snacks that use too much packaging and always pack a drink in a reusable bottle. Encourage your child to bring any uneaten food home to avoid throwing it away. If you child regularly brings food home, pack less.

6.) Don't Cook Too Much

Keep track of how much food you throw away after mealtimes. If your child consistently leaves half the food on their plate, you may need to start cooking less. Children can be picky if they don't like something or they're not very hungry so try to gauge how much you should cook by asking your child how much they might want of a meal before cooking too much.

7.) Be Clever With Arts And Crafts

Arts and crafts are a big part of a child's life. When they're small children will be entertained by painting and building structures. When they're in school they'll have art projects and other creative homework assignments. In order to create less waste, save materials like cereal boxes, string, yoghurt pots, small pieces of paper, and fabric. Encourage your child to repurpose the things you have before purchasing expensive and wasteful art supplies.

8.) Use The Library

If your child is a keen reader, consider using the public or school library rather than buying books you will later get rid of. Using the library is free and creates no waste. Alternatively, encourage your child to borrow or swap books with a friend or buy your child's books second hand. Before you buy books, ask yourself if it's a book your child will want forever, or one they'll be happy to just read and return.

9.) Make Donations
Once your children have gotten all the use they can out of clothing, shoes, books, bedding, and toys, donate them to charity or a friend in need. Art supplies, puzzles, toys, and books can be donated to local schools and youth clubs. Clothing can be handed down to a friend, relative, or a family in need. Ask other parents if they know of any charities that accept regular donations.

10.) Purchase Less
Tiny clothes and shoes are adorable but many parents over spend when it comes to baby clothes. Children grow out of their clothes very quickly so buying too many articles of clothing will usually means that half of them won't get worn. Buy second hand clothes and accept hand-me-downs wherever possible and keep shopping to a minimum.

11.) Wash Smart
Wash your baby's clothes by hand or in a short washing machine cycle. Always use a gentle laundry detergent such as a natural or homemade product. Baby clothes can get pretty dirty and washing machines use a lot of energy. Do your best to only use the washing machine when you have a full load. Use bibs to prevent having to wash an entire outfit and get a second wear out of clothes and pyjamas wherever possible.

12.) Repurpose Baby Clothes
Tiny baby clothes make great outfits for dolls and teddy bears so before you throw away your cutest little outfits, think about keeping them for Teddy! Get creative with other craft projects too such as keepsake items, homemade stuffed animals, and toddler quilts.

Getting Creative With Waste Reduction

Now that your No-Waste Home is running like a well-oiled machine, let's get to the fun stuff! This last section is all about getting crafty and creative with your waste materials. The first list here covers some clever alternatives to gift giving, wrapping paper, and gift bags. The second list includes all of my favorite no-waste craft projects.

5 Solutions To Wrapping Paper Waste

1.) Make It Count
Why give your friends and loved ones a gift wrapped in beautiful paper when they're going to look at once and then throw it away? Why not make the wrapping paper part of the gift? Think about some ways you can package your gifts in materials that can be used again. For instance try wrapping a gift in a homemade tote bag, a tee shirt, or a pillow cover! How about wrapping a few new books in a belt for a vintage look? Or some gardening tools packed in a flower pot? If you aim to make the gift wrap part of the gift you'll create less waste, show your creativity, and you might even inspire your friends to think twice about using disposable wrapping paper too!

2.) Use Found Materials
Fashion your own gift wrap with things you would've thrown away otherwise such as fabrics, tinfoil, felt, newspaper, and magazines. Throw in some paint, a nice color yarn, or some multicolored paper clips. Why spend money on wrapping paper when you can make something creative and personalized from things you already have in the house? Your friends will love it!

3.) Make A Request
If you have a birthday, wedding, or other celebration coming up, ask your friends to skip the paper when giving you a gift. They might get inspired to be creative when wrapping your gift or at least think twice about gift giving practices in the future.

4.) Reuse It

If someone presents you with a gift in wrapping paper, keep it and try to use it again in the future. You'll save money and reduce waste. And if your friends quiz you about it, use it as a platform to spread the no-waste word!

5.) Repurpose It

Use your saved gift wrap in another way. Get creative with it by covering a notebook or toy box. Use it to decorate a glass jar or fold some origami with it. Cover shelves or drawers with it. When all else fails, cut it into strips and use it for your to-do lists.

10 Creative No-Waste Craft Projects

1.) The T-Shirt Bag

Use you favorite old t-shirt to make a really cute reusable shopping bag. This is a simple project that takes very little sewing skill. There are a number of basic design patterns available online including tote bags and drawstring bags. You can use a sewing machine or sew your bag by hand. Either way, you'll love the results and you'll have an entirely unique bag!

2.) The T-Shirt Scarf

This is a simple project that can be sewn by hand or with a sewing machine. Find a few old t-shirts and any other fabrics you like. These can be old bed sheets, curtains, tablecloths, you name it! Cut the fabrics into even squares displaying your favorite parts of the fabrics and hem each square on all four sides. Next sew all the squares together in a row for a totally unique homemade scarf!

3.) The T-Shirt Quilt

If you have a lot of old t-shirts or other fabrics you love, why not make a totally creative one-off quilt? Simply cut your fabrics into even squares as seen above, hem each side of your squares, and sew together to make a quilt. Make your squares large for a bigger and less time consuming quilt project.

4.) The Cloth Organizer

Turn your unwanted bed sheets and other fabrics into a simple pocket organizer. Hang it on the bathroom door for a unique storage unit or hang it inside a kitchen cupboard to keep your cleaning products organized. Make a small one for your bedroom to store your jewellery in, or make a big one for the kids' play room!

5.) The Cushion Covers

Pillow covers are simple to make and take next to no sewing experience. They're a great way to spruce up old cushions and use fabrics that would otherwise go to waste. You can make pillow covers out of virtually any fabric and in any size. Transform an old denim jacket or favorite sweatshirt into a decorative cushion. Or use a funky pair of retro curtains to add some spice into your living room decor! If you don't like sewing, use some fabric glue for a quick fix!

6.) The Six-Pack Tool Box

Take a cardboard carrier from a six-pack and make a cute tool box, craft organizer, or condiments server. Simply reinforce the carrier with waste cardboard (I use cereal boxes and glue for this). Then paint or cover your tool box in your favorite fabric. Bed sheets, curtains, t-shirts, and just about any other fabric works well with this project. These homemade storage boxes are a great conversation starter.

7.) The Bed Sheet Hammock

You can make a hammock with as little as a bed sheet and a strong piece of rope. Decorate it by sewing other fabrics one large sheet quilt-style and display it in your back yard. Or simply fold up the sheet the way it is and bring it camping with you for an impromptu relaxation session.

8.) The Baby Mobile

When your baby grows out of their first clothes, make a few stuffed toys out of them. Draw or paint faces on them and hang them above your baby's crib to keep them amused! If your crafting skills aren't up to such a bug challenge, try just cutting a few basic shapes like stars and diamonds, sewing them together, stuffing them, and attaching engaging pictures on them.

9.) The Christmas Decorations
Use odd bits of fabric, felt, yarn, cardboard, tin foil, and ribbon to make your own Christmas decorations. Ask the kids to join you! Make birds, stars, candy canes, Santa hats, reindeer heads and whatever else you like! Decorate your home or give the decorations to friends and family!

10.) The Homemade Party
Make your get together more exciting by making some no-waste party decorations. Use your fabrics and other reusable materials to make banners, streamers, and paper chains. Make party hats out of light cardboard and tin foil. Make a "pin the tail on the donkey" game with cardboard, felt, and coloured papers. Make a table cloth out of your favorite fun fabrics. Offer your guests name cards and other party favours too!

No-Waste, Save Money, Help The Environment!

The impact of waste disposal on the environment is serious and there's no time to waste when it comes to saving our planet and protecting the health of future generations. Living in a No-Waste Home does not have to be difficult nor time consuming. Simply making a few changes to your everyday life and spreading the no-waste word could have a profound effect on the world around you. Taking waste seriously could mean more food for our fellow human beings, cleaner air and water, and less environment related illnesses. Teaching our children about proper waste disposal and encouraging them to reuse and repurpose their belongings is a necessary step for their future. At the end of it all, I promise that you will never regret making your home a No-Waste Home!

51963624R00024

Made in the USA
Middletown, DE
15 November 2017